# Exceptionally Ezra

## And the Tattle Tale

Written by: Taylor Harper

Illustrated by: Frances Rose Español

ISBN:

979-8-3304-8991-6 (sc)

Illustrations by Frances Rose Español

Layout and Design by Louie Romares

In a cozy kitchen, where
sunlight would peek,
Ezra was whisking, all
focused and sleek.
Flour flew high, as he
mixed with delight,
While Oliver, the baby,
caused quite a sight!

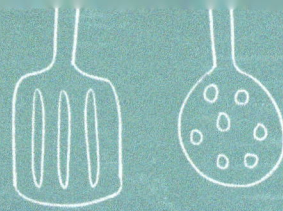

With cereal scattered from the box on the floor,
Oliver giggled, "Look, Ezra! More, more!"
As Ezra whipped cream with a flick of his wrist,
He caught a glimpse of a treat he couldn't resist.

Bake him a Cake!

"Cosmic Brownies!
Fudgy and bright,
I'll make a cookie version—
what a tasty sight!"

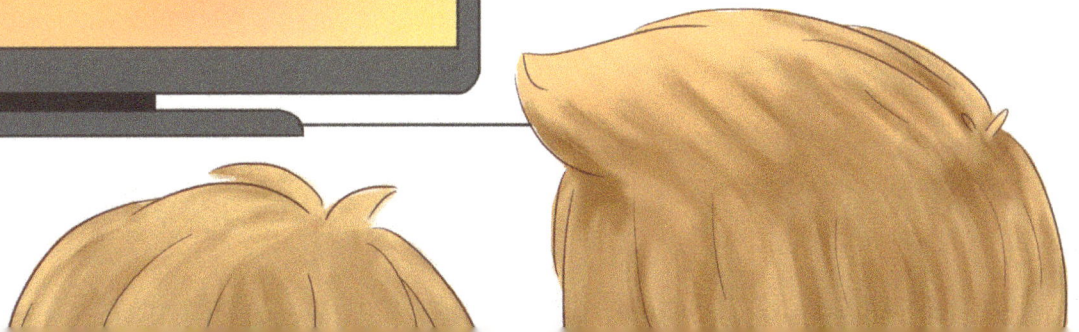

**BEST
Brownies**

But wait! Who came crawling with a giggle and glee?

It was little Oliver, as cute as can be.

"I wanna help, Ezra!
Let me stir the mix!"
Ezra sighed, "Okay, but
don't mess up my fix!"

Let's bake, Team up together for cookie's sake!" They grabbed a bowl, poured in the flour, Ezra showed Oliver how to mix with power.

Oliver stirred with tiny hands so bold, "Me help, me mix! Cookies, I'm told!" They giggled and wobbled, side by side, Baking was better with Oliver as guide!

As Ezra mixed butter, Oliver reached for a bowl,

With a splash and a splatter, it took quite a toll.

Batter flew high, like a delicious brown kite,

"Oh no, Oliver! This isn't quite right!"

The kitchen was messy, with flour in the air, Ezra gasped, "Oh no, what a sight! This isn't how I pictured my cosmic cookie night!" Oliver giggled, "I wanted to help! I'm sorry, dear brother, I didn't mean to yelp." But Ezra crossed his arms, feeling quite mad, "This was supposed to be fun, now it's just bad!" "Stop being grumpy!" Oliver pouted, But Ezra huffed, "I want you out!" Tensions rose, laughter was lost, Could they mend what was tossed?

They wrestled and yanked,
tempers on high,
The whisk slipped away
with a shared cry.

"Ugh! Why is this so hard?"
Ezra stomped with a glare.
"Because you're not listening! It just isn't fair!"

Ezra shouted Mom! We need your flair, Come help us out; we're in a flour-filled affair!" He threw up his hands, flour flying with glee, While Oliver pouted, "You always want her, me!"
"I just want to bake without all this mess, Frustration is high; it's causing me stress!" Mom peeked in, laughing at their wild scene, "What's going on, boys? You're a baking machine!"
Ezra sighed, "We're trying to bake, But it's turning into a flour explosion—what a mistake!"

m o m!!!!!!

Mom stepped in, eyes wide with surprise, "Boys, what's happening? Why the fuss and cries? The kitchen looks like a scene from a fright!" With flour on the floor and batter in sight, Ezra and Oliver were tangled in woe. "Ezra started it!" Oliver pointed, all aglow, But Ezra shot back, "He's the one being loud!" Mom raised her brows, trying not to frown, "Fighting over cookies? Let's flip this around! You both love to bake, so here's what we'll do: Together you'll create something tasty and new!"

Mom took a seat and beckoned the boys,
"Let's talk this out, and find some joys.
Baking together means teamwork instead!
You can't let a little mess fill you with dread!"

"Look at this chaos; it's all part of the fun!
You'll make a great team if you work as one.
So, take a deep breath and try once more,
Together you'll create something to adore!"

Ezra and Oliver exchanged a glance,
Realizing that maybe they'd
missed their chance.
With a nod and a smile, they
wiped off their frowns,
Ready to turn their kitchen around!

Ezra took a breath, feeling a change of heart,
He turned to Oliver, ready to restart.
"I'm sorry, little bro, for losing my cool;
I didn't mean to be mean; that's not how we rule."

Oliver crossed his arms, still feeling quite mad,
"I wanted to help more; this is just bad!"
"It's not fair," he huffed, "I'm not just a toy!"
Ezra frowned, "I know, but I want to enjoy!"

With a sigh, they stood,
tension still thick,
But deep down, they knew
they needed to fix it quick.

Oliver puffed out his cheeks, clearly quite mad,
"Ezra! Me help! This is just bad!
I wanna make cookies, not just watch on the floor!"

Ezra knelt down, trying to ease the fight,
"Okay, little buddy, let's make it all right.
I need your help; you're part of the crew,
Together we'll bake, just me and you!"

Oliver nodded, still feeling a bit sore,
"Cookies, cosmic cookies! I want to do more!"
With that, they dove in, both ready to play,
Baking together would brighten their day!

With a deep breath, Ezra smiled, feeling bright, "Alright,
little bro, let's make this right! Let's bake cosmic cookies,
side by side, I need your help; let's enjoy the ride!"
Oliver perked up, excitement aglow, "Cookies! Cosmic
cookies! I'm ready to go!" They gathered their tools, giggling
with cheer, Ready to bake, with nothing to fear.
They mixed and they laughed, joy filling the air, No more fighting—
just teamwork and care. In their messy kitchen, they found
pure delight, Creating sweet memories, oh, what a night!

With flour in the air and chocolate chips near, Ezra and Oliver were ready to cheer. They took turns mixing, measuring with glee, Making their cookies as happy as can be!

"Pour in the sprinkles!" Oliver shouted with glee, Ezra laughed, "Just a pinch—let it be!" They stirred and they giggled, a blast all around, No more mess or fuss; fun was profound!

As the dough came together, they shaped each sweet ball, Rolling and patting, they were having a ball.

"Cosmic cookies, here we come!" Ezra grinned, Together they knew this was where fun would begin!

With the cookies shaped, they placed them with care, Into the oven, filling the air. They watched through the glass, eyes wide with delight, "Look at them rising! They're such a sweet sight!" Ezra clapped hands, and Oliver jumped high, "Cosmic cookies are baking—oh my, oh my!" They gazed at their treats, golden and round, Their teamwork had turned their frowns upside down! "Can you smell that?" Ezra said with a cheer, "It's the scent of our cookies—so yummy and dear!" Oliver grinned, feeling happy and proud, "Together we did it! Let's cheer out loud!"

Mom!!!!!

Just then, they both shouted, "Mom! Come quick!"
Their voices rang out, sounding frantic and thick.
Mom rushed down the stairs, a look of surprise,
"What's going on, boys? You're not in a fight, are you guys?"

Later on the couch, with cookies in hand,
Ezra and Oliver sat, feeling quite grand.
With crumbs on their cheeks and smiles ear to ear,
They smirked at their mom, who approached with good cheer.

"Why did you call me?" she asked with a frown,
Seeing the boys munching, all cozy and brown.
"Did something go wrong? Are you two in a fight?"
But they just giggled, their eyes shining bright.

"We just wanted to share
our delicious surprise!"
Ezra grinned wide, while
Oliver tried to disguise
The cookie in his mouth as
he nodded with glee,
"Look at our cookies!
They're cosmic, you see?"

On the couch, the boys held
their cookies up high,
"Look at our cosmic treats!
They're ready to fly!"
Ezra declared proudly,
his cookie a star,
Oliver chimed in,
"Best cookies by far!"

They clinked their treats,
giggling with cheer,
"Cookie cheers!" they
shouted, voices sincere.
Mom watched, amused,
her heart feeling light,
Seeing her boys so happy,
everything felt right.

"Let's take a big
bite!" Ezra said
with a grin,
As they munched
on cookies, the
fun would begin.
With crumbs on
their laps and
joy in the air,
On that cozy
couch, they showed
love and care!

As they munched and laughed, a jingle rang clear, The cosmic brownies commercial brought them near! "Look, it's the brownies!" Oliver squealed with delight, Ezra grinned back, "Our cookies shine bright!" Mom joined the laughter, crumbs on her face, "Your cosmic cookies are winning this race!" They cheered together, their voices in tune, "Cosmic cookies for the win—let's bake again soon!" With chocolate in hand and joy all around, They savored their treats, laughter abound. In that cozy moment, with cookies galore, They knew they'd made memories to cherish and adore!

BEST
Brownies

# Cosmic Cookies

## Ingredients

½ cup unsalted butter softened
½ cup light brown sugar
¼ cup granulated sugar
1 large egg
1 teaspoon vanilla extract
2 tablespoons light corn syrup Fun fact: this is not the same thing as high fructose corn syrup!
¼ teaspoon baking soda

¼ teaspoon salt
½ cup dark cocoa powder I use Hershey's Special Dark
1 ¼ cup all-purpose flour
Toppings:
¾ cup semi-sweet chocolate chips
¼ cup heavy cream
rainbow chip sprinkles

## Method

Instructions

Preheat oven to 350°F.

In a large bowl, use an electric mixer on medium-high speed to cream softened unsalted butter (½ cup, 1 stick), light brown sugar (½ cup), and granulated sugar (¼ cup) for 2 minutes until light and fluffy. Add the egg (1 large), vanilla extract (1 teaspoon), and light corn syrup (2 tablespoons) and mix on low speed until combined. Scrape down the sides of the bowl so everything can combine. Add in baking soda (¼ teaspoon) and salt (¼ teaspoon) and mix for another 5-10 seconds until combined.

Lastly, add dark cocoa powder (½ cup) and all-purpose flour (1 ¼ cups) and mix on medium until combined. Scoop dough into ¼ cup (4 tablespoons sized scoops (I use this stainless steel cookie scoop!), roll into balls, then gently flatten each dough ball into a ½" thick disc, this will help them spread instead of be puffy. Bake at 350°F for 11-12 minutes. Do not overbake. The centers may look a tiny bit wet but will continue to bake on the hot pan, allowing them to firm up without overbaking. Allow to fully cool before decorating.

Milton Keynes UK
Ingram Content Group UK Ltd.
UKHW051555011224
451618UK00029B/16

9 798330 489916